Andrew Chipman's Christmas Angel

by Richard W. Linford

Andrew Chipman's Christmas Angel

by Richard W. Linford

First edition.

ISBN 1-57574-017-6

Imprint Linford Corporation

A Sweetwater Book Company publication

The "tuxedo" photo is provided courtesy of Mike Borrero, owner of Mike's Formal Wear, 2410 E Riverside Drive, Suite C-8A, Austin Texas 78741, 512-385-1889. Fax 512-385-1897. Email: mike@mikesformalwear.com; mikesformalwear@yahoo.com. Website: www.mikesformalwear.com

Contents

Andrew Chipman's Christmas Angel

Andrew Chipman's Christmas dream was subtle, bordering on not being there at all, occurring on Christmas Eve during semi-conscious hours just after midnight. Yet his dream was real. It was one of those dreams you might remember and mull over for nights and even days to come, wondering if it was a "legitimate" communication from the other side.

A willowy and surreal specter, much like Marley in Dickens' Christmas Carol, entered Andrew's imagination to stand at the foot of his bed, gentle, almost immobile, perhaps so as not to alarm. Andrew was not shaken by the apparition and he had no desire to wake up simply because he was immersed in this calm, warm, peaceful feeling which broadcast no sense of fear or foreboding. Some distance from Maryanne, Andrew was on his side of their king-size bed accepting this quiet, mental phantasm, listening, talking to one another by spoken thoughts not by audible spoken words.

He was a young man, thirtyish, over six-feet tall, with a light emitting aura, the mixed white and varied color light streaming especially from his smiling face. His hair was short and brown. He was dressed in a white tuxedo with white bow tie and with a pink rose in his lapel. He was smiling; yet at the same time it was obvious he was ethereally or maybe eternally serious. He said his name used to be Bill Anderson when he was on earth. He said he had practiced law in Denver where he founded and managed a large litigation law firm because of which he had gotten to know Andrew well enough to gain a more than modest respect for Andrew's tenacity, integrity and decent legal mind as a defense lawyer. Andrew knew the firm well. After Mr. Anderson's death, Andrew had applied to be a partner at the firm but had not been accepted by the surviving partners; at which point, Andrew put aside his obvious disappointment and simply continued his own private practice.

Telepathically Bill said: "Andrew, I have come to arrange to take your son, Jimmy, home. Your prayers have been monitored, and the power in charge has respects your deep-rooted faith and commitment, and HE thought it would be a great kindness to forewarn and give you notice before such action is taken involving Jimmy. Thus, through proper channels, I have been authorized to delay that action, relay this message, and spend some time visiting with you."

- - - -

Andrew did not drink alcohol, having made that decision before and then again when he was a young marine, so this visitor in a white tux was not to be attributed to one drink too many. Next day, on Christmas morning, as he read the eggnog recipe magnetized to the refrigerator door, Andrew slowly turned the concoction over in his mind; musing somewhat in personal jest that his dream could have materialized from drinking too much of Maryanne's fancy Christmas non-alcoholic eggnog. He was almost certain her half crazy eggnog brew could conjure up more than one dream or two.

Each year since they were married in the Denver Mormon Temple, on Christmas Eve, Maryanne had started and kept alive their now family tradition of serving her very own Christmas eggnog in her demitasse white "half cup" porcelain Christmas tea cups after adding her own "twist of the wrist" sprinkle of nutmeg. As well, Maryanne had conjured up a series of family toasts just for the Christmas occasion. Andrew had secretly always believed it was much easier to buy some Meadowgold Eggnog at Ben's Market. But then, making eggnog was one of Maryanne's things. It was one more of her personal contributions to their growing list of family traditions, and over the years she had kept this family eggnog tradition more than alive and well. (1)

- - - -

This first dream had not been in the least one sided. Andrew felt from the moment Bill entered his mind and disclosed his intentions that he was permitted to talk with him, man to man, to this once Bill Anderson attorney at law person. This now thirtyish looking, light emitting, tall, handsome, articulate young man in the immaculate white tux with bow tie and vest with pink rose in the lapel.

 Starting what could be Andrew's very intimidating cross examination, Andrew thought: "Why would there be any need for Jimmy on the other side that could not be filled by someone else? What could be so important as to disrupt my family?"

Not disconcerted in the least, Bill thought back his defense: "You see Jimmy as a seventeen year old mortal. You have little or no appreciation for Jimmy's real talents and abilities. In reality, Jimmy's spirit is eons old. Like all of us, Jimmy lived with The Father in pre-existent glory for eons prior to his birth into mortality. Jimmy's spirit has eternal powers you cannot understand. And Jimmy is needed by God for a special assignment. Jimmy is God's child first before he was your child."

"How critical is it for Jimmy to be the one to perform this special assignment for God? Maryanne and the other children will not recover if you take Jimmy from them, not to mention my sorrow and my loss."

"I wasn't told the answer to that question. I am only the messenger and I want you to know I too empathize with what your wife and children are about to experience, including yourself, of course."

"Will you ask the powers that be or the power that IS just how crucial it really is that Jimmy be the one to perform this special assignment?"

"I will ask," thought Bill.

"While you are asking, ask if I can substitute for Jimmy while Jimmy stays with his mom and little brother and sisters long enough for him to get married and have some kids. That way I will at least have grandchildren out of this deal. You know, continuation of my family name. When will I see you again with the answers?"

"Sooner than later; but I don't know for sure when I will visit you again because I don't make the rules. I just do as I am told."

"Do you have another "other world" name besides Bill?"

"Yes. But that name is of special relevance to me and to Him and to the others and that name has no relevance to you."

"Do you work with people on other worlds or is this the only world you deal with?"

"This is the only world," Bill thought. "Those who have lived on each particular world take care of those assigned to live on that world."

Bill left Andrew; yet when Andrew awoke, the dream was still front and center in his mind in bright, living detail – including the white tux and the pink rose.

– – – –

Christmas Eve embraced their traditional family dinner of roast beef, mashed potatoes, dark gravy, with apple pie, coupled with a fun conversation.

Then there was Maryanne's reading the nativity story, (2) and the family singing Christmas songs, and of course Maryanne's Christmas eggnog toasts.

"To the memory of baby Jesus," said Maryanne.

"To the memory of our savior and his redeeming love

 "To the memory of His holy resurrection."

"To Peter's happiness!"

"To Jimmy's happiness!"

"To Amy's happiness!"

"To Janet's happiness!"

"To Andrew's happiness!"

"To us as a family!"

Maryanne was beautiful and sensitive and Andrew was a blessed man.

 You were supposed to take just a sip with each toast so the eggnog would last, although in later years several of the grandchildren would "woof" the eggnog down and promptly ask for more.

 Christmas day there were plenty of presents, most of which were bought and wrapped by Maryanne. Andrew gave Maryanne a set of Kings Singers CDs. Maryanne made fun of his atrocious gift wrapping and the rest of Christmas day blurred together with all the other December 25ths.

After the holidays, Andrew got back in the swing of his legal work and the Christmas Eve dream almost faded from memory. Andrew was too busy dealing with an IRS failure to file criminal defense to think much about the dream, let alone analyze it; yet, whenever Jimmy came into the room, Andrew would recall the dream and think about Jimmy.

- - - -

When Jimmy was three years old, Andrew had Jimmy in his car seat in the back of their red Jaguar sedan. Andrew was waiting for Maryanne and the older kids to come out of Elitch Gardens when without warning, two swarthy looking men opened Andrew's car door, pulled Andrew from the car, pushed him to the ground, and drove off in the red Jaguar at high speed.

A young man in a Ford Mustang who was waiting behind Andrew saw the whole thing, motioned to Andrew, and the two of them sped off after the carjackers, honking and chasing them at high speeds through Denver. At one point on a main road into Englewood, the carjacker kidnappers pulled off onto the shoulder and when the Mustang pulled in behind, one of them set Jimmy down on the side of the road and jumped back in the Jaguar and sped off. Andrew picked up the crying little Jimmy and comforted him. By this time, police cars had joined the chase. The police lost the carjackers and the Jaguar was never recovered. It was no doubt metal food for some car jacker's "Gone in Sixty Seconds" chop shop.

- - - -

Then there was the Telluride San Juan Mountains, with views once enjoyed only by Ute Indians who set summer camps along the San Miguel River and hunted mountain sheep, deer and elk. There is a Mountain Lodge ski resort set between two ski runs in Telluride's Mountain Village. It has leather furniture, pine cabinetry, granite countertops, flagstone accents.

Maryanne booked a six room log and stone cabin with gourmet kitchen, private balcony, and jetted tub in the master bathroom. The lodge links to Telluride and a 13 minute ride on the lift takes you downtown. Telluride was a gold, silver, zinc, lead, and copper mining town and boasts more than 350 miles of old mine tunnels. In 1889, Butch Cassidy and his "Wild Bunch" robbed their first bank at Telluride. The San Miguel National Bank. Today the gold is in the Telluride real estate and snow skiing.

It was just above the town of Telluride where Jimmy was lost in the mountains for a day and a night after he ran off on a side trail without a word. The trail cuts parallel to the town on the side hill and after thirty minutes it petered out. The whole town of Telluride came out to look for this small blond six year old boy. Amazingly, Andrew worked with the family border collie Gretchen, and after a whole lot of backtracking and crisscrossing, the two of them found Jimmy. But it was only after Andrew's intense prayer and soul searching and promises to God.

- - - -

Jimmy played high school basketball for the Rallston Valley Mustangs with their 24 win 4 loss .857 ratio. Jimmy was all state starting point guard and was known as "little Napoleon." From the moment he got the ball he was this brilliant military basketball general in charge of the attacking troops and something electric happened.

Jimmy dribbled behind his back. He passed without looking at the other guard, forwards or center. He called plays by raising one or more fingers and at command his teammates would move, weave, and shoot. The Mustang team was top in league play. After each game, Andrew would share details with Maryanne who for some reason didn't attend the games and never got excited about sports even though Jimmy was this amazing All State star point guard.

Andrew had watched the first Rallston Englewood pre-league game and the much smaller Englewood players played defense like madmen and won handily. Andrew thought the Englewood team had played as perfect a game as possible; but then Jimmy was suffering some kind of dysentery or flu and sat the bench during that game.

At the first league game, though, Englewood never had a chance. When Jimmy was on the floor it was like the basket for the Englewood team had a lid on it. Rallston held the

Englewood team scoreless first quarter and third and fourth quarters. Englewood made most of its points second quarter. But Jimmy didn't play second quarter. When Jimmy played, he set up a defense that shut the Englewood team down and at the opposite end Rallston poured in shots from every possible angle. During one period, Jimmy made four three point shots in a row.

- - - -

After the game, Andrew got permission from the coach to drive Jimmy home.

"You played well, son," Andrew said as understatement.

"Thanks, Dad," said Jimmy.

"Anything on your mind you want to talk about?"

"Not really," said Jimmy.

"Doing well in your studies?"

"Getting A's and one A minus."

"Congratulations. What's the A minus in?"

"English."

"Why the minus?"

"Missed one assignment. Mrs. Gambol says I can make it up by writing a paper if I want to."

"Do you want to?"

"Probably."

"Well, whatever you do is ok with me."

"I know."

"How's your physical health?"

"No problems that I know of."

"Mental health?"

"Same."

"Spiritual health? Any problems with pornography or girls?"

"No problems, Dad."

Alone with a son in the car was a good time for Dad and son conversations like this.

"Want to drive through and get a milkshake?"

"Sure."

"Hamburger?"

"Sure."

Andrew took the raspberry double malt and a hamburger and Jimmy the Cookie dough milk shake, cheeseburger and fries.

- - - -

The accident was as unexpected as the Rallston win was expected.

The pickup was traveling parallel in the left lane, passing Andrew and Jimmy on the freeway. The patrolman estimated the Ford F-150 was going at least 95 miles per hour when the driver lost control, veered off into a wide grassy semi-flat median area, overcorrected, came back up onto the freeway, except now the truck was traveling across the freeway perpendicular to and in front of Andrew and Jimmy.

The truck grazed the front bumper of Andrew's Lincoln, skidded erratically for at least 150 feet on the right shoulder, only to strike a metal barricade with enough force to roll the truck in the grassy area to the right of the freeway.

Andrew and Jimmy watched in fear and amazement as truck and driver rolled round and round and though the truck was totaled the seat belted intoxicated driver climbed out of the truck having only sustained a sprained wrist. With serious effort, Andrew kept control of their Lincoln.

"I'm grateful for you son. Are you all right?"

"Yes," said Jimmy. "I'm grateful for you too, Dad. Are you all right?"

"Yes. That was a close one."

"Way too close!" Jimmy said.

- - - -

Notwithstanding the close call and the tedious wait for the patrolmen to finish their paperwork, that February night when Andrew crawled in bed, he was still feeling euphoric over Jimmy's basketball game until Bill entered Andrew's dream thoughts again.

It was the same quiet, calm, peace again. Bill stood at the foot of the bed. Once more he was dressed in the white tux with the pink rose in the lapel and he was still emitting this incredible light from his aura and especially from his face and out the top of his head. And he was still smiling.

"I have some answers to your questions," Bill thought.

"What are they? Andrew thought.

"They discussed your comments and questions in a patient and reasonable manner. Everyone was most gracious."

"Who is everyone?" thought Andrew.

"Everyone is all who are on my committee including my supervisor. The word is Jimmy is not the only person who can perform the assignment. Also, there is an inordinate amount of empathy for what Maryanne and your other children would face were Jimmy taken right now. So I have it on good authority. If you would like, you can substitute for Jimmy for a few years while Jimmy stays with the family. Everyone is in agreement.

"Jimmy will get married and have a family and follow in your footsteps as a defense attorney. I was told who Jimmy's wife will be and who their children will be, so you are guaranteed more than one grand child including a couple of grandsons who will continue your name. Someone is needed to fill the assignment, though; and the choice is yours, Andrew."

"The choice is mine?"

"Yes. The choice is yours."

When do you need me?" thought Andrew.

"Eleven months," thought Bill. "The latest day this assignment can be filled is next Christmas day, December 25th."

"May I think about it for a few days?" Andrew thought. "I didn't expect to see you again. I gave up on our first dream as the by product of Maryanne's Christmas eggnog. It isn't often you have back to back dreams like this replete with angel in white tux with a pink rose in his lapel. Nothing like this has ever happened to me before."

"Certainly," Bill thought. "I will talk to you again. Do you have any other questions right now?"

"Questions?"

"Yes, questions."

"Well now that you ask, what is it like?" Andrew thought.

"What is what like?"

"You know. What is it like on the other side?"

"I'm not sure I can describe it to you, Andrew."

"Why?"

"Because it is so far beyond your knowledge or experience base or imagination," thought Bill.

"Try me. And do all you guys wear white tuxes?"

"No, they don't all wear white tuxes like I do. Most wear and enjoy the robe. I'm dressed this way so you will relate and feel happy and comfortable."

"I would feel much more comfortable if you wore levis or khakis and a long sleeve shirt and a pull over sweater and loafers."

"I'll keep that in mind."

"At least try to tell me what it is really like?"

- - - -

"Well, if I say it is beautiful and peaceful, what does that mean to you? No war. No military establishment. No nuclear or other arms. No contention. No ill will. Only the finest feelings of Christ-like love and happiness creating an atmosphere of peace in the extreme. No blaring media with its incessant sex and violence. Paradise is simply a complete expression of everlasting peace and love where everyone helps and lifts each other.

"If I were to tell you that the air and the panoramic views and the animals and the plants and the mansions and the personal interactions are so spectacular there is nothing here on earth with which to compare them, what does that mean to you? Lions eating grass side by side with lambs. All of the animals you know and some others you can't imagine, all living together in harmony. There are cherries, apples, and fruits you can't even conceive of and the tree of life with "pure love of Christ" fruit so white and delicious. Our living quarters are not only made of light, they are filled with light.

"If I were to say there is no sickness, pain, death, or sorrow, no envy or sin, no crime or corruption on the other side in Paradise, what does that mean to you? If I say you can download more knowledge on multiple subjects in seconds – more knowledge and wisdom than it would take you here on earth a lifetime to learn, what does that mean to you? For one thing, and you will probably find this humorous, I will tell you that contrary to the opinion of many on earth that most lawyers belong in hell, there are many, many lawyers in paradise." (3)

"You have got to be kidding," thought Andrew.

"No, I am not kidding! In fact, Andrew, I don't kid. It is now contrary to my nature to lie. Next to the teachers, the legal profession is one of the largest professions on the other side. There are no doctors in Paradise because there is no sickness and there are no policemen because there is no crime and no firemen because there is no fire and no stock brokers because there is no stock since everyone has everything in common. But there are architects and builders who give oversight to mansion construction and there are many, many defense and prosecuting attorneys."

"You really have got to be kidding. Are there any lawyer jokes?" Andrew wisecrack thought." Maybe you heard this one when you were mortal. The story is told of a Doctor who went to a brain store to get some brain to complete a medical study. He sees a sign remarking on the quality of professional brains offered for sale so he begins to question the butcher about the cost of each of the brains. 'How much does it cost for an ounce of engineer brain?' 'Three dollars an ounce.' 'How much for software programmer's brain?' 'Five dollars an ounce.' 'How much for lawyer brain.' 'One thousand dollars an ounce.' 'Why so much more for an ounce of lawyer brain?' 'Took a lot more lawyers to make up one ounce of brain!'

"Funny. On occasion there is a good lawyer joke or two on the other side. The humor there really is quite amusing and it doesn't rely on canned laughter tracks like you have on your comedy TV shows," thought Bill.

"On a serious note," thought Andrew, "I have read that Jesus Christ is our Advocate with the Father. Isn't he our judge as well?" (4)

"Yes, but those are simplistic statements, Andrew. It is true Our Savior worked out the atoning sacrifice in our behalf and provides the grace we need to overcome the sins and mistakes we make in mortality, of course conditional on our faith in Him and our repentance of our sins and our enduring to the end in continuing good works.

"Yet, there is a highly active and complex judicial system in place in paradise. You receive a time. You show up on your court date. You meet before one or more judges who may in some cases serve as a panel of judges.

"Your pre-earth life and your mortal life are downloaded from your memory banks and from the book of life. Your mortal life is shown to those present in living color with surround sound in an intimate comfortable setting by means of a remarkably interactive set of holographic visions. It takes several hours calculated in earth time to review and judge a life.

"I hasten to say that as a kindness from Our Supreme Judge and Savior, where one has repented and truly changed, those sins and mistakes are not included in this life's holographic documentary. This makes for some interesting and often humorous viewing because it is sometimes difficult to splice together seamlessly the many "repentance" gaps in a person's life. Anyway, after all of that you receive a sentence from your judge or panel of judges. **(5)**

"A sentence?"

"Yes, a sentence. You are judged and sentenced to a particular reward or set of rewards or assignments and to a specific mansion." **(6)**

"Sort of like the story of John Weightman in Henry Van Dyke's story *The Mansion*? John spent his life amassing wealth and giving it away as a philanthropist and when John went to heaven he found that his mansion was tiny in the extreme compared to the mansions of those who had given of themselves in quiet humble service to others? John received his big reward on earth and his miniscule reward in heaven?" **(7)**

"Sort of. The John Weightman story is extremely primitive. It is also a simplistic description of the judgment. In truth, the Plan of Salvation including the judgment on the other side is far more complex and comprehensive than you can imagine. It is much more detailed. It is much more analytical. It is much more probing.

"On the same hand, the gospel and the great plan of happiness and judgment are much more loving, gracious, merciful and kind than you can imagine. And at times as I said it can be very humorous. On the other hand, it is perfectly accurate and absolutely fair and just, more so than you can imagine.

"When Christ says His Father cannot look upon sin with the least degree of allowance, that is exactly what He means. Within this "other world" judgment system, the corollary is a maxim that in his mercy, perfect love and kindness, as I said, He will not look upon repentant sin as sin at all.

"The judgment is the most amazing, ultimate teaching and learning experience. And you can attend on your own and where necessary plead your own case, or if you are smart you will have an "other world" advocate like me to represent you and help you plead your case. **(8)**

"Perhaps that is why I have been asked to visit with you in these dreams. Most of my time has not been spent with my family and friends or in downloading more knowledge about the galaxy and the universe. Most of my eternal time since my death has been spent defending men and women at their judgment hearings.

"Like I said, you can attend on your own and defend yourself or you can have someone like me help defend you if you would like. There is also a comprehensive set of appeals in place and they are somewhat technical so more often than not it is very helpful to have someone like me as an advocate. You didn't think the Savior would conduct all of the judicial hearings by himself did you?"

"I hadn't thought about it."

"Most in mortality haven't thought about it either, so it comes as quite a surprise and shock. I like the word simplistic when it comes to the gospel. There is a lot of simplistic thinking going on among you mortals. If you read the scriptures at all, you usually gloss over a scripture and you don't take the time to analyze it and plumb it to its depths and more often than not you don't take it literally, which in most cases it is.

"Jesus Christ is our advocate with the Father in the sense that he gives oversight to the judicial process. He serves as the ultimate judge, and of course he is the one who is even higher than the Apostolic Supreme Court. He is present only during the most extremely difficult and compelling appellate cases.

"In a poor comparison, yet one which you can relate to, the primary judgment process has been delegated to the Supreme Court which is made up of his Apostles, and to a series of lower courts made up of his bishops and other ecclesiastical officers. Within paradise there are several different levels of appellate courts." (8)

"I thought each person is judged immediately at the time of death by Christ?"

"It is true there is an immediate partial judgment as described in Matthew 25. If you were a decent person and you cared for the poor and the needy, you are assigned to Paradise, which is a place of peace and happiness. If you did not care for the poor and the needy, you are assigned to a place that has been described as a spirit prison, an area within the spirit world which is very confining and mentally painful to those who have not lived moral, decent, righteous lives.

"After that initial judgment or "separation," the expanded judgment process is implemented wherein a person is rewarded for his or her righteous thoughts, desires, words and actions when compared with the light, truth, and knowledge he or she was given and achieved in mortality. And rewards differ dramatically. As you might surmise, one of my rewards has been my great pleasure and good fortune of visiting with you and tutoring you about things to come. **(9)**

"Can we do this again?"

"We can. At least we can until I am told not to visit you again."

"When would you like to meet again?" thought Andrew.

"I will let you know. I have to return and report the details of our discussion. As I told you, I am expected and required to be meticulous in doing only as I am told."

- - - -

When Andrew rehearsed his first dream to Maryanne, she expressed only a mild concern. This second dream was another matter. Now she would really think he was nuts. When Maryanne went walking next morning, Andrew got out of bed late, took the twenty steps to his bathroom, dressed, and then stepped into his office, which was a converted bedroom right next to the bathroom. Andrew checked his email and made his daily to-do list.

Andrew spent his days doing legal work for a number of clients, preparing for and teaching Sunday school, and now and then visiting family. He was also trying to write his first novel. Somehow, much of the legal work he had done during past years didn't seem to be of much value. In some respects, Andrew felt sort of like he had been climbing the wrong tree in the forest, a tree not tall enough to afford much of a view of the valley or mountains or beyond. Even at his age, Andrew wondered if he had lived and would continue to live the right kind of life. When he "came to die," in the words of Henry David Thoreau, Andrew did not want to die only to "discover that he had not lived." And Andrew did not wish to "live what was not life, since living is so dear." **(10)**

- - - -

A week later Andrew sat in his family room watching a picture-in-picture Denver Broncos football game on his 67 inch HDTV. He was simultaneously watching another program while taping several programs. He had earlier acquired the recording system so it was easy to watch a couple of shows and at the same time look at the menu and record a football game or an action or western or war movie, or a great musical or theatrical performance which usually were far and few between. Andrew counted this recording system as one of his most important purchases. He, Maryanne and the kids could be protected from the sex and violence. He could high speed past commercials and any raw or inane content.

Andrew had begun to watch a taped and fairly violent Law and Order show when Maryanne walked in. She was his second conscience and would not watch shows carrying violence or sex or anything inane. He had observed that she had long since graduated to a higher state of personal conduct and perfection. She watched religious channels or the news or politics once in a while or a decent Masterpiece theater play, or a Gershwin concert, anything in the Apostle Paul's category of "virtuous, lovely, of good report and praiseworthy." When she entered the room, she saw Andrew was watching the dark, violent episode of Law and Order so she quietly turned and walked away.

Andrew called to her. "Do you want to watch with me?"

"Yes. But ..."

Andrew interrupted. "I recorded a NOVA about the Milky Way."

Maryanne came back in the room, took a blanket, curled up on the couch, and was soon fast asleep as was her usual reaction to most shows. She didn't sleep well at night, suffering from sleep apnea or some sleep malady. But without fail she could sleep in front of most any TV show.

The NOVA documentary was mind blowing. Billions of galaxies. Trillions of stars. Four hundred billion stars estimated in our own Milky Way Galaxy. Multiple colors reflecting off space dust clouds. Distances and possibilities reaching lightyears into the future and into the past.

Andrew thought, "How is it possible for God to number and name and keep everything straight? Who are we and what is our destiny? Where do we come from? Andrew thought about the fact that inside of thirty years he would die and pass into another realm of existence to his rewards whatever they might be. "From eternity to all eternity" the scriptures say. **(11)**

During the show, Andrew kept thinking that he had not told Maryanne about his second encounter of the third kind or whatever you might want to call it. Another dream from "another world?" he thought.

A sobering messenger from heaven dressed in a white tux with white tie and a pink rose in his lapel? In fact, Andrew's dreams were downright disconcerting. Was it even possible such communications from paradise could happen? Andrew stayed awake long after Maryanne had gone to sleep. He would tell her in the morning. "Maybe I need to see a shrink," he thought. "Maybe I have a brain tumor or slow hemorrhage or some strange mental disorder." But then he mumbled to himself that Maryanne was a shrink. She was a non-practicing psychiatrist.

- - - -

Sometime around two a.m., Andrew fell asleep and Bill entered his mind again.

"You have some added questions?" Bill thought.

Andrew thought: "I do have questions. First let me say I agree to substitute for Jimmy starting December 25th."

"That is right noble of you," Bill thought.

"I don't know how noble it is. I only know it is the right thing to do, but obviously my view of the universe is from my limited perspective. I will be leaving Maryanne and my kids prematurely. My Uncles lived until they were in their late nineties. My dad lived until he was ninety three. So I've got longevity genes built into my chromosomes and I should live for a long time to come," Andrew thought, knowing full well that it was of no importance to Bill to hear these facts.

"It is still noble of you. Sacrifice is noble and enobling. The months will pass by quickly," thought Bill.

- - - -

"I want to know the answers to questions like: do people get married in the "other world?" What do you do for entertainment? What are your homes like? What do you eat or do you eat? Do you have any contact with Heavenly Father or is he far away on His celestial world? Can you travel between the worlds? And should I tell Maryanne?"

"Slow down. One question at a time. Do people marry in the "other world? Don't you know the answer to that question intuitively? Of course they do. As only one illustration, how else would you have millions of women or men who don't have a chance to marry in this life get married if they don't marry in the "other world?" This is a common sense answer which everyone ought to know intuitively. Relationships there are very much like relationships here except in Paradise they are coupled with an overwhelming abundance of Christ-like selfless love and affection and there is no infidelity or immorality or envy or unkindness.

"Regarding our entertainment? Think of the best, the finest, the most uplifting and moving concert or show you have ever attended and then add most any multiple you can think of and you have amazing combined music, dance, drama, and holographic visual and participatory experiences.

"As for our homes, they are nothing like what you live in here in mortality. As I mentioned to you earlier, the homes are made of light and they literally build themselves from architectural plans. And yes we do eat the finest food imaginable. And Heavenly Father is on His celestial world. And for a few, there is travel between the worlds. But for the most part we have plenty to do in helping those who have lived and live and will yet live on this world. Tell Maryanne? Of course! Why would you not tell Maryanne?

- - - -

Andrew tried to rehearse his life altering dream experiences to Maryanne who listened in silence, slowly processing, as she was wont to do. She didn't roll her eyes. She said nothing. The idea of a trade of Jimmy's life for Andrew's life was poignant for her and Andrew could see tears in her eyes. Maryanne really did love Andrew. In a paraphrase of Golda's words from Fiddler on the Roof, she had washed his clothing, made his bed, and cooked his meals. She had suffered his inability to lose weight. She had put up with his mannerisms. She had dealt with his moments of uncouth or forgetfulness or lack of empathy and thoughtfulness. She had laughed at his weak jokes. She had slept with him all these years. She had born and raised these great children. She had watched him suffer when she had suffered through her bout with breast cancer. She had suffered with him when he lost his multi-million dollar business at the same time as the 9-11 twin tower disaster. Of course, she loved him. **(12)**

In all this she admired his great qualities. His integrity. Whenever he helped her. His love for their children. His intelligence. Whenever he protected her. His obvious love for her. She had earned her "Putting Hubby Through (PHT)" degree by helping him through law school. He had reciprocated by putting her through medical school. In doing so, he earned his "Putting Wifa Through (PWT)" degree. Andrew made that one up.

If that's not love, what is love? Andrew thought. **(12)**

Do you have any headaches? "No."

Have you bumped your head getting into the car? "No."

Have you fallen recently? "No."

Maryanne probed.

She knew severe head injuries cause personality changes and in some instances result in schizophrenia and psychotic symptoms.

Are you on any medications I don't know about beyond your daily small aspirin? "No."

Have you been eating well? "Yes."

"Are you going through a post mid-life crisis? "No."

Are you depressed or anxious? "No."

Is there some traumatic or abusive past or current experience you are suppressing and trying to deal with? "No."

Have you prayed about these dream experiences? "Yes."

Well, what do you make of them?

"They are all too real," Andrew replied. "They are all too real."

"If one happens again, wake me up," Maryanne said.

One happened again but not for several months and Andrew did not wake Maryanne up. It happened on the night of November 4th to be precise. Actually, during a small hour of the morning at 4:15 am to be even more precise. Andrew groggily stole a look at the clock.

- - - -

During the last ten months, Andrew had gone out of the way not to be ordinary or ornery.

He continued to help his law clients but with an added level of personal service, helping young people pro bono.

He attended church and to the best of his ability each day and each week repented of his sins and changed for the better.

He took time to prepare and he made extra mile serious effort to teach his Sunday School class.

He read in the Bible and The Book of Mormon more often than he had before his first encounter with Bill last Christmas.

He prayed a whole lot more intensely.

Everything about his life was several steps above the old ordinary, ornery Andrew.

He had several dates with Maryanne each month when the past experience had been for the two of them to go out together only once every few months.

Andrew went out of his way to be much more helpful to Maryanne and his neighbors and his children.

And he made it a point to increase their Church offerings.

He gave away his camel hair coat to a poor young man during a snow storm and did not tell Maryanne or anyone else about it.

Nothing showy. No radical changes. But clearly not the "same old same old Andrew," he thought.

He worried about anyone he might have offended in the past and Andrew prayed for them and for himself.

He had a long standing habit of reviewing and repenting of his sins each night and especially each Sunday during sacrament meeting before he took the sacrament.

Andrew had in general made his peace with God.

Both at home and in his law practice, Andrew went well out of his way to be a peacemaker and to be helpful to his clients.

In fact, peacemaker was a good definition of Andrew the lawyer. Andrew simply kept up with the tedious process of enduring to the end. He thought often of his Christmas bargain, exchanging his life for Jimmy's, the consummation of which was now only 55 days away.

- - - -

"You seem so distant," Maryanne said.

"Distant?" Andrew asked.

They were walking through the neighborhood.

They were holding hands.

"Distant! Pre-occupied! Pensive! Off on another world! Far away!" she raised her voice at him.

"I'm sorry."

"You are thinking about those dreams, aren't you?"

"Yes!" He could not lie to her.

"Have you had another one recently you haven't told me about?

"No." He lied and then caught himself. "Yes!"

"Didn't you promise me you would tell me?"

"Yes."

Maryanne launched into her psychiatric commentary and interrogation.

"You know such dreams can be caused by stress."

"Yes."

"I know you have significant stress in your life. Being a defense attorney is no cakewalk. Tell me about some of your cases over the last four years."

"Over the last four years?"

"Yes."

"Well, I defended one fellow for failure to file. That matter has taken up a great deal of my time and mental energy during the past four years. You know about that one. I defended a client who is a heavy meth user. I defended three teenagers accused of theft. I defended a client who has been addicted to oxycontin. I helped structure a number of merger and acquisition business deals, several of which were aborted."

"And you have taken me through breast cancer treatment."

"Yes."

"And you have watched one of your close friends die from esophageal cancer."

"Yes."

"And your Dad died."

"Yes."

"And your mother had a stroke and then died in a care facility."

"Yes."

"And your brother was in heart failure and had heart surgery."

"Yes."

"And you lost a multi-million dollar business."

"Yes."

"And your partner abandoned you and didn't lift a finger to help."

"Yes."

"I would say you have had your share of reasons to be stressed and have a couple of strange dreams. I love you, Andrew. I admire how well you have been able to cope with your heavy load."

"Do you think you have significant stress in your life, Andrew?"

"I suppose so."

"But do you really think so?"

"You know, I think all of this is just part of a good day's work." Andrew said.

"Yeh, sure! And I'm Princess Diana, too!" Maryanne was just getting warmed up.

"Andrew, some of my psychiatrist colleagues think dreams are random mind noise during one's sleep and have no real meaning.

"Others key into the Freudian analysis and delve into and probe deeply into a dreamer's sexual psyche."

"I do not doubt for a minute that certain dreams are complex and have religious significance but there is no Daniel in The Lion's Den manual I can use to interpret your dreams."

"There is some evidence that a dream series can prelude an onset of mental illness."

" Andrew, I want to have you checked out this week. It is better to take care of things while they are small and fixable. Maybe you need some medication to get rid of your stress load. Maybe you just need a vacation. Aside from our St. George trip, the last time we took a real solid multi-week vacation together was several years ago."

" And besides, Andrew, you still need to lose twenty or thirty pounds!" Maryanne was raising her "you're fat not fit" voice.

When she called him Andrew, it meant she was getting hot under the collar and bothered and exercised about his health and well being and invariably she ended on the weight thing and said "Andrew!" using his name emphatically and almost in vain.

- - - -

The fourth interview occurred the very same night as their walk.

"This is the last time I will visit with you," thought Bill.

"Why is that?" thought Andrew.

"I have another assignment."

"Oh. I thought you were going to visit me off and on right up until December 25th?"

"I thought there would be another visit or two with you as well." said Bill. "Andrew, you have been reassigned to three other persons during the days prior to your transition."

"Three more defense lawyers?" Andrew continued without waiting for the answer. "I knew it."

"Knew what?"

"Defense lawyers! All defense lawyers are nuts like me."

Bill smiled. "You're not nuts, Andrew. Those three other persons are not defense lawyers, Andrew. They are your Dad and two grandpas. Do you have any more questions?"

Andrew felt himself brushing away tears with the back of his hand.

"A couple of questions."

"What are they?" thought Bill.

"What do you think will cause my death?" thought Andrew.

"Your heart will give out and I predict you won't feel a thing. You won't notice the transition from mortality to eternal life at all. It will feel natural.

"Out of body. Walking toward the light. Embraced by the light. Perfect peace and comfort. These phrases don't even begin to define the experience of dying. You will honestly enjoy the experience. What is your second question?"

"What will happen to Maryanne?

"I thought you would ask. She will be very well taken care of. You have provided a good block of insurance. She will have no inclination to remarry. She will follow you not too long after." thought Bill.

"Then what will I be doing on the other side? thought Andrew.

"My committee thought you would ask that question too. I've been assigned to serve as your supervisor. If you are still willing to substitute for a couple of years, you will take Jimmy's place and serve as one of the seven defense lawyers on my team? You will be making visits to others like I have been visiting with you and assuming they agree you will be providing the defense on their behalf," thought Bill. "The work is very satisfying."

"Does this mean you will conduct my defense? I probably need the best defense lawyer I can find."

"Yes, I will be glad to conduct your defense if you want me to."

"And how long do I get to rest before my court date?" thought Andrew.

"You will have an orientation first. Then you ought to be able to rest for a couple of earth months until your hearing." thought Bill.

"After my hearing, do I get to choose who I help? Assuming I pass my judgment, that is," thought Andrew.

"In His service there is always a choice!" thought Bill.

"And Andrew, there is no question in my mind that you will pass your exam and receive a very enjoyable reward."

"Have you worked through the details of leaving your kids and Maryanne? You have your will and trust? Some savings? A decent amount of life insurance? Other income to care for Maryanne and the children?"

"Yes." thought Andrew.

"And do you really accept? thought Bill.

Even though he was asleep, Andrew was keenly aware that he was again wiping tears from his eyes with the back of his hand. "Yes, I really do accept," thought Andrew. "Better me than Jimmy right now. And I really will miss Maryanne desperately," thought Andrew.

"I know. And she will miss you too. I also know and assure you she will be all right with this," thought Bill. "There is an eternal law of compensation and the blessings will come. Sacrifice always brings forth the blessings of heaven."

"I will stop by with your Dad and grandpas and pick you up on December 25th. We are scheduled to be at your place promptly at 11:30 pm. That way you can spend Christmas day with your family."

"I'll be waiting," thought Andrew.

Footnotes

(Footnote 1) Maryanne's Eggnog recipe without any alcohol? See the
Internet for eggnog recipes.

(Footnote 2) Nativity Story. King James Version of the Bible?

LUKE CHAPTER 2

Angelic ministrants herald the birth of Jesus in Bethlehem—He is
circumcised, and Simeon and Anna prophesy of his mission— At twelve
years he is about his Father's business.

1 AND it came to pass in those days, that there went out a decree from
Caesar Augustus, that all the world should be taxed.

2 (*And* this taxing was first made when Cyrenius was governor of Syria.)

3 And all went to be taxed, every one into his own city.

4 And Joseph also went up from Galilee, out of the city of Nazareth, into
Judaea, unto the city of David, which is called Bethlehem; (because he
was of the house and lineage of David:)

5 To be taxed with Mary his espoused wife, being great with child.

6 And so it was, that, while they were there, the days were
accomplished that she should be delivered.

7 And she brought forth her firstborn son, and wrapped him in
swaddling clothes, and laid him in a manger; because there was no room
for them in the inn.

8 And there were in the same country shepherds abiding in the field,
keeping watch over their flock by night.

9 And, lo, the angel of the Lord came upon them, and the glory of the Lord shone round about them: and they were sore afraid.

10 And the angel said unto them, Fear not: for, behold, I bring you good tidings of great joy, which shall be to all people.

11 For unto you is born this day in the city of David a Saviour, which is Christ the Lord.

12 And this *shall be* a sign unto you; Ye shall find the babe wrapped in swaddling clothes, lying in a manger.

13 And suddenly there was with the angel a multitude of the heavenly host praising God, and saying,

14 Glory to God in the highest, and on earth peace, good will toward men.

15 And it came to pass, as the angels were gone away from them into heaven, the shepherds said one to another, Let us now go even unto Bethlehem, and see this thing which is come to pass, which the Lord hath made known unto us.

16 And they came with haste, and found Mary, and Joseph, and the babe lying in a manger.

17 And when they had seen *it,* they made known abroad the saying which was told them concerning this child.

18 And all they that heard *it* wondered at those things which were told them by the shepherds.

19 But Mary kept all these things, and pondered *them* in her heart.

20 And the shepherds returned, glorifying and praising God for all the things that they had heard and seen, as it was told unto them.

21 And when eight days were accomplished for the circumcising of the child, his name was called JESUS, which was so named of the angel before he was conceived in the womb.

22 And when the days of her purification according to the law of Moses were accomplished, they brought him to Jerusalem, to present *him* to the Lord;

23 (As it is written in the law of the Lord, Every male that openeth the womb shall be called holy to the Lord;)

24 And to offer a sacrifice according to that which is said in the law of the Lord, A pair of turtledoves, or two young pigeons.

25 And, behold, there was a man in Jerusalem, whose name *was* Simeon; and the same man *was* just and devout, waiting for the consolation of Israel: and the Holy Ghost was upon him.

26 And it was revealed unto him by the Holy Ghost, that he should not see death, before he had seen the Lord's Christ.

27 And he came by the Spirit into the temple: and when the parents brought in the child Jesus, to do for him after the custom of the law,

28 Then took he him up in his arms, and blessed God, and said,

29 Lord, now lettest thou thy servant depart in peace, according to thy word:

30 For mine eyes have seen thy salvation,

31 Which thou hast prepared before the face of all people;

32 A light to lighten the Gentiles, and the glory of thy people Israel.

33 And Joseph and his mother marvelled at those things which were spoken of him.

34 And Simeon blessed them, and said unto Mary his mother, Behold, this *child* is set for the fall and rising again of many in Israel; and for a sign which shall be spoken against;

35 (Yea, a sword shall pierce through thy own soul also,) that the thoughts of many hearts may be revealed.

36 And there was one Anna, a prophetess, the daughter of Phanuel, of the tribe of Aser: she was of a great age, and had lived with an husband seven years from her virginity;

37 And she *was* a widow of about fourscore and four years, which departed not from the temple, but served *God* with fastings and prayers night and day.

38 And she coming in that instant gave thanks likewise unto the Lord, and spake of him to all them that looked for redemption in Jerusalem.

39 And when they had performed all things according to the law of the Lord, they returned into Galilee, to their own city Nazareth.

40 And the child grew, and waxed strong in spirit, filled with wisdom: and the grace of God was upon him.

41 Now his parents went to Jerusalem every year at the feast of the passover.

42 And when he was twelve years old, they went up to Jerusalem after the custom of the feast.

43 And when they had fulfilled the days, as they returned, the child Jesus tarried behind in Jerusalem; and Joseph and his mother knew not *of it*.

44 But they, supposing him to have been in the company, went a day's journey; and they sought him among *their* kinsfolk and acquaintance.

45 And when they found him not, they turned back again to Jerusalem, seeking him.

46 And it came to pass, that after three days they found him in the temple, sitting in the midst of the doctors, both hearing them, and asking them questions.

47 And all that heard him were astonished at his understanding and answers.

48 And when they saw him, they were amazed: and his mother said unto him, Son, why hast thou thus dealt with us? behold, thy father and I have sought thee sorrowing.

49 And he said unto them, How is it that ye sought me? wist ye not that I must be about my Father's business?

50 And they understood not the saying which he spake unto them.

51 And he went down with them, and came to Nazareth, and was subject unto them: but his mother kept all these sayings in her heart.

52 And Jesus increased in wisdom and stature, and in favour with God and man.

MATTHEW CHAPTER 2

The wise men are directed by a star to Jesus—Joseph takes the child to Egypt—Herod slays the children in Bethlehem—Jesus is taken to Nazareth to dwell.

1 Now when Jesus was born in Bethlehem of Judaea in the days of Herod the king, behold, there came wise men from the east to Jerusalem,

2 Saying, Where is he that is born King of the Jews? for we have seen his star in the east, and are come to worship him.

3 When Herod the king had heard *these things,* he was troubled, and all Jerusalem with him.

4 And when he had gathered all the chief priests and scribes of the people together, he demanded of them where Christ should be born.

5 And they said unto him, In Bethlehem of Judaea: for thus it is written by the prophet,

6 And thou Bethlehem, *in* the land of Juda, art not the least among the princes of Juda: for out of thee shall come a Governor, that shall rule my people Israel.

7 Then Herod, when he had privily called the wise men, enquired of them diligently what time the star appeared.

8 And he sent them to Bethlehem, and said, Go and search diligently for the young child; and when ye have found *him,* bring me word again, that I may come and worship him also.

9 When they had heard the king, they departed; and, lo, the star, which they saw in the east, went before them, till it came and stood over where the young child was.

10 When they saw the star, they rejoiced with exceeding great joy.

11 ¶ And when they were come into the house, they saw the young child with Mary his mother, and fell down, and worshipped him: and when they had opened their treasures, they presented unto him gifts; gold, and frankincense, and myrrh.

12 And being warned of God in a dream that they should not return to Herod, they departed into their own country another way.

13 And when they were departed, behold, the angel of the Lord appeareth to Joseph in a dream, saying, Arise, and take the young child and his mother, and flee into Egypt, and be thou there until I bring thee word: for Herod will seek the young child to destroy him.

14 When he arose, he took the young child and his mother by night, and departed into Egypt:

15 And was there until the death of Herod: that it might be fulfilled which was spoken of the Lord by the prophet, saying, Out of Egypt have I called my son.

16 ¶ Then Herod, when he saw that he was mocked of the wise men, was exceeding wroth, and sent forth, and slew all the children that were in Bethlehem, and in all the coasts thereof, from two years old and under, according to the time which he had diligently enquired of the wise men.

17 Then was fulfilled that which was spoken by Jeremy the prophet, saying,

18 In Rama was there a voice heard, lamentation, and weeping, and great mourning, Rachel weeping *for* her children, and would not be comforted, because they are not.

19 ¶ But when Herod was dead, behold, an angel of the Lord appeareth in a dream to Joseph in Egypt,

20 Saying, Arise, and take the young child and his mother, and go into the land of Israel: for they are dead which sought the young child's life.

21 And he arose, and took the young child and his mother, and came into the land of Israel.

22 But when he heard that Archelaus did reign in Judaea in the room of his father Herod, he was afraid to go thither: notwithstanding, being warned of God in a dream, he turned aside into the parts of Galilee:

23 And he came and dwelt in a city called Nazareth: that it might be fulfilled which was spoken by the prophets, He shall be called a Nazarene.

(Footnote 3) Paradise?

LDS BIBLE DICTIONARY DEFINITION OF THE WORD PARADISE

"A Persian word meaning *a garden*. It is not found in the Old Testament. In the New Testament it occurs in Luke 23:43, 2 Corinthians 12:4, and Revelation 2:7. See also Book of Mormon 2 Nephi 9:13; Alma 40:12, 14; 4 Nephi 1:14; Moroni 10:24; Doctrine &Covenants 77:2,5; cf. Articles of Faith 10. Paradise is that part of the spirit world in which the righteous spirits who have departed from this life await the resurrection of the body. It is a condition of happiness and peace. However, the scriptures are not always consistent in the use of the word, especially in the Bible. For example, when Jesus purportedly said to the thief on the cross, "To day shalt thou be with me in Paradise" (Luke 23:43)), the Bible rendering is incorrect. The statement would more accurately read, "Today shalt thou be with me in the world of spirits" since the thief was not ready for paradise (see History of the Church of Jesus Christ of Latter-day Saints 5: 424-25). Possibly 2 Corinthians 12:4 should also not use paradise in the sense of meaning the spirit world, as much as meaning the celestial kingdom. The "paradisiacal glory" of Articles of Faith 10 refers to the glorified millennial state of the earth rather than the spirit world.

(Footnote 4) Jesus Christ is our Advocate with the Father?

1. 1 John 2:1

   1 My little children, these things write I unto you, that ye sin not. And if any man sin, we have **an advocate with the Father**, Jesus Christ the righteous:

2. LDS Scripture, Doctrine & Covenants 29:5

   5 Lift up your hearts and be glad, for I am in your midst, and am your **advocate with the Father**; and it is his good will to give you the kingdom.

3. Doctrine & Covenants 45:3

   3 Listen to him who is the **advocate** with **the Father**, who is pleading your cause before him—

4. Doctrine & Covenants 110:4

   4 I am the first and the last; I am he who liveth, I am he who was slain; I am your **advocate with the Father**.

(Footnote 5) Jesus Christ is the Supreme Judge and Savior. He assigns other judges.

1. LDS Book of Mormon, 3 Nephi 27:14-16, 25-277

    14 And my Father sent me that I might be lifted up upon the cross; and after that I had been lifted up upon the cross, that I might draw all men unto me, that as I have been lifted up by men **even so should men be lifted up by the Father, to stand before me, to be judged of their works, whether they be good or whether they be evil—**

    15 And for this cause have I been lifted up; therefore, according to the power of the Father I will draw all men unto me, **that they may be** judged **according to their works.**

51

16 And it shall come to pass, that whoso repenteth and is baptized in my name shall be filled; and if he endureth to the end, behold, him will I hold guiltless before my Father at that day when **I shall stand to** judge **the world.**

• • •

25 For behold, **out of the books which have been written, and which shall be written, shall this people be judged, for by them shall their works be known unto men.**

26 And behold, all things are written by the Father; therefore **out of the books which shall be written shall the world be** judged.

27 And know ye that **ye shall be judges of this people**, according to the judgment which I shall give unto you, which shall be just. Therefore, what manner of men ought ye to be? Verily I say unto you, even as I am.

Doctrine & Covenants 64:11, 37-38

11 And ye ought to say in your hearts—**let God judge between me and thee, and reward thee according to thy deeds.**

• • •

37 Behold, I, the Lord, have made my church in these last days like unto a judge sitting on a hill, or in a high place, **to judge the nations.**

38 For it shall come to pass that **the inhabitants of Zion shall judge all things pertaining to Zion.**

2. John 8:15-16, 26

    15 Ye judge after the flesh; I judge no man.

    16 And yet if I judge, my judgment is true: for I am not alone, but I and the Father that sent me.

    • • •

    26 **I have many things to say and to judge of you**: but he that sent me is true; and I speak to the world those things which I have heard of him.

3. Romans 14: 3, 10, 14

    3 Let not him that eateth despise him that eateth not; and let not him which eateth not [a]**judge** him that eateth: for God hath received him.

    • • •

    10 **But why dost thou judge thy brother? or why dost thou set at nought thy brother? for we shall all stand before the judgment seat of Christ.**

    • • •

    13 Let us not therefore **judge** one another any more: but **judge** this rather, that no man put a stumblingblock or an occasion to fall in *his* brother's way.

4. Book of Mormon, Mormon 3:18-20

18 Yea, behold, I write unto all the ends of the earth; yea, unto you, **twelve tribes of Israel, who shall be judged according to your works by the twelve whom Jesus chose to be his disciples in the land of Jerusalem.**

19 And I write also unto **the remnant of this people, who shall also be judged by the twelve whom Jesus chose in this land; and they shall be judged by the other twelve whom Jesus chose in the land of Jerusalem.**

20 And these things doth the Spirit manifest unto me; therefore I write unto you all. And for this cause I write unto you, that ye may know **that ye must all stand before the judgment-seat of Christ, yea, every soul who belongs to the whole human family of Adam; and ye must stand to** be **judged of your works, whether they be good or evil;**

5. Psalm 9: 4, 8, 19

4 For thou hast maintained my right and my cause; thou satest in the throne **judging** right.

• • •

8 **And he shall judge the world in righteousness, he shall minister judgment to the people in uprightness.**

• • •

19 **Arise, O LORD; let not man prevail: let the heathen be** judged **in thy sight.**

6. Ezekiel 7:3, 8, 27

   3 Now *is* the end *come* upon thee, and I will send mine anger upon thee, **and will judge thee according to thy ways, and will recompense upon thee all thine abominations.**

   • • •

   8 Now will I shortly pour out my fury upon thee, and accomplish mine anger upon thee: and **I will judge thee according to thy ways, and will recompense thee for all thine abominations.**

   • • •

   27 The king shall mourn, and the prince shall be clothed with desolation, and the hands of the people of the land shall be troubled: I will do unto them after their way, and according to their deserts will I **judge** them; and they shall know that I *am* the LORD.

(Footnote 6) Men are judged and rewarded for their righteousness or for their evil?

1. Book of Mormon, Alma 9:28

   Therefore, prepare ye the way of the Lord, for the time is at hand that all men **shall reap a reward of their works, according to that which they have been—if they have been righteous they shall reap the salvation of their souls, according to the power and deliverance of Jesus Christ; and if they have been evil they shall reap the damnation of their souls, according to the power and captivation of the devil.**

55

(Footnote 7) Ending to the story of John Weightman by Henry van Dyke?

"Where do you wish me to lead you now?"

"To see my own mansion," answered the man, with half-concealed excitement. "Is there not one here for me? You may not let me enter it yet,
perhaps, for I must confess to you that I am only--"

"I know," said the Keeper of the Gate--"I know it all.
You are John Weightman."

"Yes," said the man, more firmly than he had spoken at first,
for it gratified him that his name was known. "Yes, I am John Weightman, Senior Warden of St. Petronius' Church. I wish very much to see
my mansion here, if only for a moment. I believe that you have
one for me. Will you take me to it?"

The Keeper of the Gate drew a little book from the breast of his
robe and turned over the pages.

"Certainly," he said, with a curious look at the man, "your name
is here; and you shall see your mansion if you will follow me."

It seemed as if they must have walked miles and miles, through
the vast city, passing street after street of houses larger and
smaller, of gardens richer and poorer, but all full of beauty and delight.

They came into a kind of suburb, where there were many small
cottages, with plots of flowers, very lowly, but bright and fragrant.
Finally they reached an open field, bare and lonely-looking.
There were two or three little bushes in it, without flowers,
and the grass was sparse and thin. In the center of the field
was a tiny hut, hardly big enough for a shepherd's shelter.
It looked as if it had been built of discarded things, scraps and
fragments of other buildings, put together with care and pains,
by some one who had tried to make the most of cast-off material.

There was something pitiful and shamefaced about the hut.
It shrank and drooped and faded in its barren field, and seemed
to cling only by sufferance to the edge of the splendid city.

"This," said the Keeper of the Gate, standing still and speaking
with a low, distinct voice--"this is your mansion, John Weightman."

An almost intolerable shock of grieved wonder and indignation
choked the man for a moment so that he could not say a word.
Then he turned his face away from the poor little hut
and began to remonstrate eagerly with his companion.

"Surely, sir," he stammered, "you must be in error about this.
There is something wrong--some other John Weightman--a confusion
of names--the book must be mistaken."

"There is no mistake," said the Keeper of the Gate, very calmly;
"here is your name, the record of your title and your possessions
in this place."

"But how could such a house be prepared for me," cried the man, with a resentful tremor in his voice--"for me, after my long and faithful service? Is this a suitable mansion for one so well known and devoted? Why is it so pitifully small and mean?
Why have you not built it large and fair, like the others?"

"That is all the material you sent us."

"What!"

"We have used all the material that you sent us," repeated the Keeper of the Gate.

"Now I know that you are mistaken," cried the man, with growing earnestness, "for all my life long I have been doing things that must have supplied you with material. Have you not heard that I have built a school-house; the wing of a hospital; two--yes, three--small churches, and the greater part of a large one, the spire of St. Petro--"

The Keeper of the Gate lifted his hand.

"Wait," he said; "we know all these things. They were not ill done. But they were all marked and used as foundation for the name and mansion of John Weightman in the world. Did you not plan them for that?"

"Yes," answered the man, confused and taken aback, "I confess that I thought often of them in that way. Perhaps my heart was set upon that too much. But there are other things--my endowment for the college--my steady and liberal contributions to all the established charities--my support of every respectable--"

"Wait," said the Keeper of the Gate again. "Were not all these carefully recorded on earth where they would add to your credit?

They were not foolishly done. Verily, you have had your reward for them. Would you be paid twice?"

"No," cried the man, with deepening dismay, "I dare not claim that. I acknowledge that I considered my own interest too much. But surely not altogether. You have said that these things were not foolishly done. They accomplished some good in the world. Does not that count
for something?"

"Yes," answered he Keeper of the Gate, "it counts in the world--where you counted it. But it does not belong to you here. We have saved
and used everything that you sent us. This is the mansion prepared for you."

As he spoke, his look grew deeper and more searching, like a flame of fire. John Weightman could not endure it. It seemed to strip him naked and wither him. He sank to the ground under a crushing weight of shame, covering his eyes with his hands and cowering face downward upon the stones. Dimly through the trouble of his mind he felt their hardness and coldness.

"Tell me, then," he cried, brokenly, "since my life has been so little worth, how came I here at all?"

"Through the mercy of the King"--the answer was like the soft tolling of a bell.

"And how have I earned it?" he murmured.

"It is never earned; it is only given," came the clear, low reply.

"But how have I failed so wretchedly," he asked, "in all the purpose of my life? What could I have done better? What is it that counts here?"

"Only that which is truly given," answered the bell-like voice. Only that good which is done for the love of doing it. Only those plans in which the welfare of others is the master thought. Only those labors in which the sacrifice is greater than the reward. Only those gifts in which the giver forgets himself."

The man lay silent. A great weakness, an unspeakable despondency and humiliation were upon him. But the face of the Keeper of the Gate was infinitely tender as he bent over him.

"Think again, John Weightman. Has there been nothing like that in your life?"

"Nothing," he sighed. "If there ever were such things, it must have been long ago--they were all crowded out--I have forgotten them."

There was an ineffable smile on the face of the Keeper of the
Gate, and his hand made the sign of the cross over the bowed head as he
spoke gently:

"These are the things that the King never forgets; and because
there were a few of them in your life, you have a little place
here."

The sense of coldness and hardness under John Weightman's hands
grew sharper and more distinct. The feeling of bodily weariness
and lassitude weighed upon him, but there was a calm, almost a
lightness, in his heart as he listened to the fading vibrations of the
silvery bell-tones. The chimney clock on the mantel had just
ended the last stroke of seven as he lifted his head from the table.
Thin, pale strips of the city morning were falling into the room
through the narrow partings of the heavy curtains.

What was it that had happened to him? Had he been ill? Had he
died and come to life again? Or had he only slept, and had his soul gone
visiting in dreams? He sat for some time, motionless, not lost, but
finding himself in thought. Then he took a narrow book from the table
drawer,
wrote a check, and tore it out.

He went slowly up the stairs, knocked very softly at his son's
door, and, hearing no answer, entered without noise. Harold was
asleep, his bare arm thrown above his head, and his eager face relaxed in
peace. His father looked at him a moment with strangely shining eyes,
and then tiptoed quietly to the writing-desk, found a pencil and
a sheet of paper, and wrote rapidly:

"My dear boy, here is what you asked me for; do what you like with it, and ask for more if you need it. If you are still thinking of that work with Grenfell, we'll talk it over to-day after church.

I want to know your heart better; and if I have made mistakes--"

A slight noise made him turn his head. Harold was sitting up in bed with wide-open eyes.

"Father!" he cried, "is that you?"

"Yes, my son," answered John Weightman; "I've come back--I mean I've come up--no, I mean come in--well, here I am, and God give us a good Christmas together."

(Footnote 8) Plan of Salvation; Death, Physical; Death, Spiritual; Resurrection; Eternal Life; Kingdoms of Glory: Celestial, Terrestrial, Telestial, Perdition; Justice; Mercy; Second Coming; Millennium. See www.lds.org and www.mormon.org. These are in large measure unique teachings of The Prophet Joseph Smith.

Pre-earth Life?

"Our life before we were born on this earth. In our pre-earth life, we lived in the presence of our Heavenly Father as His spirit children. We did not have a physical body.

Plan of Salvation?

"In the premortal existence, Heavenly Father prepared a plan to enable us to become like Him and receive a fulness of joy. The scriptures refer to this plan as "the plan of salvation" (Alma 24:14; Moses 6:62), "the great plan of happiness" (Alma 42:8), "the plan of redemption" (Jacob 6:8;

Alma 12:30), and "the plan of mercy" (Alma 42:15). The plan of salvation is the fulness of the gospel. It includes the Creation, the Fall, the Atonement of Jesus Christ, and all the laws, ordinances, and doctrines of the gospel. Moral agency, the ability to choose and act for ourselves, is also essential in Heavenly Father's plan. Because of this plan, we can be perfected through the Atonement, receive a fulness of joy, and live forever in the presence of God. Our family relationships can last throughout the eternities.

Death, Physical?

"Physical death is the separation of the spirit from the mortal body. The Fall of Adam brought physical death into the world (see Moses 6:48). Because of the Atonement and Resurrection of Jesus Christ, all mankind will be resurrected and redeemed from physical death.

"Death is an essential part of Heavenly Father's plan of salvation (see 2 Nephi 9:6). In order to become like our Eternal Father, we must experience death and later receive perfect, resurrected bodies.

"When the physical body dies, the spirit continues to live. In the spirit world, the spirits of the righteous "are received into a state of happiness, which is called paradise, a state of rest, a state of peace, where they shall rest from all their troubles and from all care, and sorrow" (Alma 40:12). A place called spirit prison is reserved for "those who [have] died in their sins, without a knowledge of the truth, or in transgression, having rejected the prophets" (D&C 138:32). The spirits in prison are "taught faith in God, repentance from sin, vicarious baptism for the remission of sins, the gift of the Holy Ghost by the laying on of hands, and all other principles of the gospel that [are] necessary for them to know" (D&C 138:33–34). If they accept the principles of the gospel, repent of their sins, and accept ordinances performed in their behalf in temples, they will be welcomed into paradise.

"Because of the Atonement and Resurrection of Jesus Christ, physical death is only temporary: "As in Adam all die, even so in Christ shall all be made alive" (1 Corinthians 15:22). Everyone will be resurrected, meaning that every person's spirit will be reunited with his or her body—"restored to their proper and perfect frame" and no longer subject to death (Alma 40:23; see also Alma 11:44–45).

Death, Spiritual?

"Spiritual death is separation from God. The scriptures teach of two sources of spiritual death. The first source is the Fall, and the second is our own disobedience. Spiritual death can be overcome through the Atonement of Jesus Christ and by obedience to His gospel.

"The Book of Mormon prophet Samuel taught, "All mankind, by the fall of Adam being cut off from the presence of the Lord, are considered as dead, both as to things temporal and to things spiritual" (Helaman 14:16). During our life on the earth, we are separated from God's presence. Through the Atonement, Jesus Christ redeems everyone from this spiritual death. Samuel testified that the Savior's Resurrection "redeemeth all mankind from the first death—that spiritual death. . . . Behold, the resurrection of Christ redeemeth mankind, yea, even all mankind, and bringeth them back into the presence of the Lord" (Helaman 14:16–17). The prophet Lehi taught that because of the Atonement, "all men come unto God; wherefore, they stand in the presence of him, to be judged of him according to the truth and holiness which is in him" (2 Nephi 2:10).

"Further spiritual death comes as a result of our own disobedience. Our sins make us unclean and unable to dwell in the presence of God (see Romans 3:23; Alma 12:12-16, 32; Helaman 14:18; Moses 6:57). Through the Atonement, Jesus Christ offers redemption from this spiritual death, but only when we exercise faith in Him, repent of our sins, and obey the principles and ordinances of the gospel (see Alma 13:27–30; Helaman 14:19; Articles of Faith 1:3).

Resurrection?

"Because of the Fall of Adam and Eve, we are subject to physical death, which is the separation of the spirit from the body. Through the Atonement of Jesus Christ, all people will be resurrected and saved from physical death (see 1 Corinthians 15:22). Resurrection is the reuniting of the spirit with the body in an immortal state, no longer subject to disease or death.

"The Savior was the first person on this earth to be resurrected. The New Testament contains several accounts testifying that He rose from the tomb (see Matthew 28:1–8; Mark 16:1–14; Luke 24:1–48; John 20:1–29; 1 Corinthians 15:1–8; 2 Peter 1:16–17).

"When the resurrected Lord appeared to His Apostles, He helped them understand that He had a body of flesh and bones. He said, "Behold my hands and my feet, that it is I myself: handle me, and see; for a spirit hath not flesh and bones, as ye see me have" (Luke 24:39). He also appeared to the Nephites after His Resurrection (see 3 Nephi 11:10–17).

"At the time of the resurrection, we will "be judged according to [our] works. . . . We shall be brought to stand before God, knowing even as we know now, and have a bright recollection of all our guilt" (Alma 11:41, 43). The eternal glory we receive will depend on our faithfulness. Although all people will be resurrected, only those who have come unto Christ and partaken of the fulness of His gospel will inherit exaltation in the celestial kingdom.

"An understanding and testimony of the resurrection can give us hope and perspective as we experience the challenges, trials, and triumphs of life. We can find comfort in the assurance that the Savior lives and that through His Atonement, "he breaketh the bands of death, that the grave shall have no victory, and that the sting of death should be swallowed up in the hopes of glory" (Alma 22:14).

Eternal Life?

"Eternal life is the phrase used in scripture to define the quality of life that our Eternal Father lives. The Lord declared, "This is my work and my glory—to bring to pass the immortality and eternal life of man" (Moses 1:39). Immortality is to live forever as a resurrected being. Through the Atonement of Jesus Christ, everyone will receive this gift. Eternal life, or exaltation, is to live in God's presence and to continue as families (see D&C 131:1–4). Like immortality, this gift is made possible through the Atonement of Jesus Christ. However, to inherit eternal life requires our "obedience to the laws and ordinances of the Gospel" (Articles of Faith 1:3).

"When we are baptized and receive the gift of the Holy Ghost, we enter the path that leads to eternal life. The prophet Nephi taught:

"The gate by which ye should enter is repentance and baptism by water; and then cometh a remission of your sins by fire and by the Holy Ghost.

"And then are ye in this strait and narrow path which leads to eternal life; yea, ye have entered in by the gate; ye have done according to the commandments of the Father and the Son; and ye have received the Holy Ghost, which witnesses of the Father and the Son, unto the fulfilling of the promise which he hath made, that if ye entered in by the way ye should receive" (2 Nephi 31:17–18).

"Nephi emphasized that after we have entered this "strait and narrow path," we must endure to the end in faith:

"After ye have gotten into this strait and narrow path, I would ask if all is done? Behold, I say unto you, Nay; for ye have not come thus far save it were by the word of Christ with unshaken faith in him, relying wholly upon the merits of him who is mighty to save.

"Wherefore, ye must press forward with a steadfastness in Christ, having a perfect brightness of hope, and a love of God and of all men. Wherefore, if ye shall press forward, feasting upon the word of Christ, and endure to the end, behold, thus saith the Father: Ye shall have eternal life" (2 Nephi 31:19–20).

"After we are baptized and receive the gift of the Holy Ghost, much of our progress toward eternal life depends on our receiving other ordinances of salvation: for men, ordination to the Melchizedek Priesthood; for men and women, the temple endowment and marriage sealing. When we receive these ordinances and keep the covenants that accompany them, we prepare ourselves to inherit eternal life

Kingdoms of Glory?

"Through the Atonement of Jesus Christ, all people will be resurrected. After we are resurrected, we will stand before the Lord to be judged according to our desires and actions. Each of us will accordingly receive an eternal dwelling place in a specific kingdom of glory. The Lord taught this principle when He said, "In my Father's house are many mansions" (John 14:2).

"There are three kingdoms of glory: the celestial kingdom, the terrestrial kingdom, and the telestial kingdom. The glory we inherit will depend on the depth of our conversion, expressed by our obedience to the Lord's commandments. It will depend on the manner in which we have "received the testimony of Jesus" (D&C 76:51; see also D&C 76:74, 79, 101).

Celestial Kingdom?

"The celestial kingdom is the highest of the three kingdoms of glory. Those in this kingdom will dwell forever in the presence of God the Father and His Son Jesus Christ. This should be your goal: to inherit celestial glory and to help others receive that great blessing as well. Such a goal is not achieved in one attempt; it is the result of a lifetime of righteousness and constancy of purpose.

"The celestial kingdom is the place prepared for those who have "received the testimony of Jesus" and been "made perfect through Jesus the mediator of the new covenant, who wrought out this perfect atonement through the shedding of his own blood" (D&C 76:51, 69). To inherit this gift, we must receive the ordinances of salvation, keep the commandments, and repent of our sins. For a detailed explanation of those who will inherit celestial glory, see Doctrine and Covenants 76:50–70; 76:92–96.

"In January 1836 the Prophet Joseph Smith received a revelation that expanded his understanding of the requirements to inherit celestial glory. The heavens were opened to him, and he saw the celestial kingdom. He marveled when he saw his older brother Alvin there, even though Alvin had died before receiving the ordinance of baptism. (See D&C 137:1–6.) Then the voice of the Lord came to the Prophet Joseph:

"All who have died without a knowledge of this gospel, who would have received it if they had been permitted to tarry, shall be heirs of the celestial kingdom of God; "Also all that shall die henceforth without a knowledge of it, who would have received it with all their hearts, shall be heirs of that kingdom;

"For I, the Lord, will judge all men according to their works, according to the desire of their hearts" (D&C 137:7–9).

"Commenting on this revelation, the Prophet Joseph said, "I also beheld that all children who die before they arrive at the years of accountability are saved in the celestial kingdom of heaven" (D&C 137:10).

"From another revelation to the Prophet Joseph, we learn that there are three degrees within the celestial kingdom. To be exalted in the highest degree and continue eternally in family relationships, we must enter into "the new and everlasting covenant of marriage" and be true to that covenant. In other words, temple marriage is a requirement for obtaining the highest degree of celestial glory. (See D&C 131:1–4.) All who are worthy to enter into the new and everlasting covenant of marriage will have that opportunity, whether in this life or the next.

Terrestrial Kingdom?

"Those who inherit terrestrial glory will "receive of the presence of the Son, but not of the fulness of the Father. Wherefore, they are bodies terrestrial, and not bodies celestial, and differ in glory as the moon differs from the sun" (D&C 76:77–78). Generally speaking, individuals in the terrestrial kingdom will be honorable people "who were blinded by the craftiness of men" (D&C 76:75). This group will include members of the Church who were "not valiant in the testimony of Jesus" (D&C 76:79). It will also include those who rejected the opportunity to receive the gospel in mortality but who later received it in the postmortal spirit world (see D&C 76:73–74). To learn more about those who will inherit terrestrial glory, see Doctrine and Covenants D&C 76:71–80, 91, 97.

Telestial Kingdom?

"Telestial glory will be reserved for individuals who "received not the gospel of Christ, neither the testimony of Jesus" (D&C 76:82). These individuals will receive their glory after being redeemed from spirit prison, which is sometimes called hell (see D&C 76:84, D&C 76:106). A detailed explanation of those who will inherit telestial glory is found in Doctrine and Covenants 76:81–90, 98–106, 109–112.

Perdition?

"Some people will not be worthy to dwell in any kingdom of glory. They will be called "the sons of perdition" and will have to "abide a kingdom which is not a kingdom of glory" (D&C 76:32; 88:24). This will be the state of "those who know [God's] power, and have been made partakers thereof, and suffered themselves through the power of the devil to be overcome, and to deny the truth and defy [God's] power" (D&C 76:31; see also D&C 76:30, 32–49).

Justice?

"In scriptural terms, justice is the unchanging law that brings consequences for actions. Because of the law of justice, we receive blessings when we obey God's commandments. The law of justice also demands that a penalty be paid for every sin we commit.

"When the Savior carried out the Atonement, He took our sins upon Himself. He was able to "answer the ends of the law" (2 Nephi 2:7) because He subjected Himself to the penalty that the law required for our sins. In doing so, He "satisfied the demands of justice" and extended mercy to everyone who repents and follows Him (see Mosiah 15:9; Alma 34:14–16). Because He has paid the price for our sins, we will not have to suffer that punishment if we repent (see D&C 19:15–20).

Mercy?

"Mercy is the compassionate treatment of a person greater than what is deserved, and it is made possible through the Atonement of Jesus Christ. Our Heavenly Father knows our weaknesses and sins. He shows mercy when He forgives us of our sins and helps us return to dwell in His presence.

"God's compassion may seem to conflict with the law of justice, which requires that no unclean thing be permitted to dwell with Him (see 1 Nephi 10:21). But the Atonement of Jesus Christ made it possible for God to "be a perfect, just God, and a merciful God also" (Alma 42:15).

"The Savior satisfied the demands of justice when He stood in our place and suffered the penalty for our sins. Because of this selfless act, the Father can mercifully withhold punishment from us and welcome us into His presence. To receive the Lord's forgiveness, we must sincerely repent of our sins. As the prophet Alma taught, "Justice exerciseth all his demands, and also mercy claimeth all which is her own; and thus, none but the truly penitent are saved" (Alma 42:24; see also Alma 42:22–23, 25).

"Forgiveness of sin is not the only gift of mercy from Heavenly Father and Jesus Christ. Every blessing we receive is an act of mercy, more than we could ever merit on our own. Mormon taught, "All things which are good cometh of Christ; otherwise men were fallen, and there could no good thing come unto them" (Moroni 7:24). For example, we are recipients of divine mercy when Heavenly Father hears and answers our prayers, when we receive guidance from the Holy Ghost, and when we are healed from sickness through priesthood power. Although all such blessings come as results of our obedience, we could never receive them through our efforts alone. They are merciful gifts from a loving and compassionate Father.

"Speaking to His disciples, the Savior commanded: "Be ye . . . merciful, as your Father also is merciful" (Luke 6:36). We can follow our Heavenly Father's example of mercy in our relationships with others. We can strive to rid our life of arrogance, pride, and conceit. We can seek ways to be compassionate, respectful, forgiving, gentle, and patient, even when we are aware of others' shortcomings.

Second Coming of Jesus Christ?

"As Jesus Christ ascended into heaven at the completion of His mortal ministry, two angels declared to His Apostles, "This same Jesus, which is taken up from you into heaven, shall so come in like manner as ye have seen him go into heaven" (Acts 1:11). Since that time, believers have looked forward to the Second Coming of Jesus Christ.

"When the Savior comes again, He will come in power and glory to claim the earth as His kingdom. His Second Coming will mark the beginning of the Millennium.

"The Second Coming will be a fearful, mournful time for the wicked, but it will be a day of peace for the righteous. The Lord declared:

"They that are wise and have received the truth, and have taken the Holy Spirit for their guide, and have not been deceived—verily I say unto you, they shall not be hewn down and cast into the fire, but shall abide the day.

"And the earth shall be given unto them for an inheritance; and they shall multiply and wax strong, and their children shall grow up without sin unto salvation.

"For the Lord shall be in their midst, and his glory shall be upon them, and he will be their king and their lawgiver" (D&C 45:57–59).

"The Lord has not revealed exactly when He will come again: "The hour and the day no man knoweth, neither the angels in heaven, nor shall they know until he comes" (D&C 49:7). But He has revealed to His prophets the events and signs that will precede His Second Coming. Among the prophesied events and signs are:

- Apostasy from gospel truth (see Matthew 24:9–12; 2 Thessalonians 2:1–3).
-
- The Restoration of the gospel, including the restoration of the Church of Jesus Christ (see Acts 3:19–21; Revelation 14:6–7; D&C 45:28; 133:36).
- The restoration of priesthood keys (see Malachi 4:5–6; D&C 110:11–16).
- The coming forth of the Book of Mormon (see Isaiah 29:4–18; 3 Nephi 21:1–11).
- The preaching of the gospel throughout the world (see Matthew 24:14).
- A time of wickedness, war, and turmoil (see Matthew 24:6–7; 2 Timothy 3:1–7; D&C 29:17; 45:26–33; 88:91).
- Signs in heaven and on the earth (see Joel 2:30–31; Matthew 24:29–30; D&C 29:14–16; 45:39□42; 49:23; D&C 88:87–90).

"The righteous need not fear the Second Coming or the signs that precede it. The Savior's words to His Apostles apply to all who prepare for His coming and who look forward to it with joy: "Be not troubled, for, when all these things shall come to pass, ye may know that the promises which have been made unto you shall be fulfilled" (D&C 45:35).

Millennium?

"A millennium is a period of 1,000 years. When we speak of "the Millennium," we refer to the 1,000 years following the Savior's Second Coming (see Revelation 20:4; D&C 29:11). During the Millennium, "Christ will reign personally upon the earth" (Articles of Faith 1:10).

"The Millennium will be a time of righteousness and peace on the earth. The Lord has revealed that "in that day the enmity of man, and the enmity of beasts, yea, the enmity of all flesh, shall cease" (D&C 101:26; see also Isaiah 11:6–9). Satan will be "bound, that he shall have no place in the hearts of the children of men" (D&C 45:55; see also Revelation 20:1–3).

"During the Millennium, all people on the earth will be good and just, but many will not have received the fulness of the gospel. Consequently, members of the Church will participate in missionary work.

"Members of the Church will also participate in temple work during the Millennium. The Saints will continue to build temples and receive ordinances in behalf of their kindred dead. Guided by revelation, they will prepare records of their ancestors all the way back to Adam and Eve.

"Complete righteousness and peace will continue until the end of the 1,000 years, when Satan "shall be loosed for a little season, that he may gather together his armies." The armies of Satan will fight against the hosts of heaven, who will be led by Michael, or Adam. Satan and his followers will be defeated and cast out forever. (See D&C 88:111–115.)

2. LDS Scripture, Doctrine & Covenants 127:4

4 And again, verily thus saith the Lord: Let the work of my temple, and all the works which I have appointed unto you, be continued on and not cease; and let your diligence, and your perseverance, and patience, and your works be redoubled, and you shall in nowise lose your **reward**, saith the Lord of Hosts. And if

they persecute you, so persecuted they the prophets and **righteous men** that were before you. **For** all this there is a **reward** in heaven.

(Footnote 9) Parables of the ten virgins, the talents, and the sheep and the goats? MATTHEW 25:1-45.

MATTHEW CHAPTER 25

Jesus gives the parables of the ten virgins, the talents, and the sheep and the goats.

1 THEN shall the kingdom of heaven be likened unto ten virgins, which took their lamps, and went forth to meet the bridegroom.

2 And five of them were wise, and five *were* foolish.

3 They that *were* foolish took their lamps, and took no oil with them:

4 But the wise took oil in their vessels with their lamps.

5 While the bridegroom tarried, they all slumbered and slept.

6 And at midnight there was a cry made, Behold, the bridegroom cometh; go ye out to meet him.

7 Then all those virgins arose, and trimmed their lamps.

8 And the foolish said unto the wise, Give us of your oil; for our lamps are gone out.

9 But the wise answered, saying, *Not so;* lest there be not enough for us and you: but go ye rather to them that sell, and buy for yourselves.

10 And while they went to buy, the bridegroom came; and they that were ready went in with him to the marriage: and the door was shut.

11 Afterward came also the other virgins, saying, Lord, Lord, open to us.

12 But he answered and said, Verily I say unto you, I know you not.

13 Watch therefore, for ye know neither the day nor the hour wherein the Son of man cometh.

14 ¶ For *the kingdom of heaven is* as a man travelling into a far country, *who* called his own servants, and delivered unto them his goods.

15 And unto one he gave five talents, to another two, and to another one; to every man according to his several ability; and straightway took his journey.

16 Then he that had received the five talents went and traded with the same, and made *them* other five talents.

17 And likewise he that *had received* two, he also gained other two.

18 But he that had received one went and digged in the earth, and hid his lord's money.

19 After a long time the lord of those servants cometh, and reckoneth with them.

20 And so he that had received five talents came and brought other five talents, saying, Lord, thou deliveredst unto me five talents: behold, I have gained beside them five talents more.

21 His lord said unto him, Well done, *thou* good and faithful servant: thou hast been faithful over a few things, I will make thee ruler over many things: enter thou into the joy of thy lord.

22 He also that had received two talents came and said, Lord, thou deliveredst unto me two talents: behold, I have gained two other talents beside them.

23 His lord said unto him, Well done, good and faithful servant; thou hast been faithful over a few things, I will make thee ruler over many things: enter thou into the joy of thy lord.

24 Then he which had received the one talent came and said, Lord, I knew thee that thou art an hard man, reaping where thou hast not sown, and gathering where thou hast not strawed:

25 And I was afraid, and went and hid thy talent in the earth: lo, *there* thou hast *that is* thine.

26 His lord answered and said unto him, *Thou* wicked and slothful servant, thou knewest that I reap where I sowed not, and gather where I have not strawed:

27 Thou oughtest therefore to have put my money to the exchangers, and *then* at my coming I should have received mine own with usury.

28 Take therefore the talent from him, and give *it* unto him which hath ten talents.

29 For unto every one that hath shall be given, and he shall have abundance: but from him that hath not shall be taken away even that which he hath.

30 And cast ye the unprofitable servant into outer darkness: there shall be weeping and gnashing of teeth.

31 ¶ When the Son of man shall come in his glory, and all the holy angels with him, then shall he sit upon the throne of his glory:

32 And before him shall be gathered all nations: and he shall separate them one from another, as a shepherd divideth *his* sheep from the goats:

33 And he shall set the sheep on his right hand, but the goats on the left.

34 Then shall the King say unto them on his right hand, Come, ye blessed of my Father, inherit the kingdom prepared for you from the foundation of the world:

35 For I was an hungred, and ye gave me meat: I was thirsty, and ye gave me drink: I was a stranger, and ye took me in:

36 Naked, and ye clothed me: I was sick, and ye visited me: I was in prison, and ye came unto me.

37 Then shall the righteous answer him, saying, Lord, when saw we thee an hungred, and fed *thee?* or thirsty, and gave *thee* drink?

38 When saw we thee a stranger, and took *thee* in? or naked, and clothed *thee?*

39 Or when saw we thee sick, or in prison, and came unto thee?

40 And the King shall answer and say unto them, Verily I say unto you, Inasmuch as ye have done *it* unto one of the least of these my brethren, ye have done *it* unto me.

41 Then shall he say also unto them on the left hand, Depart from me, ye cursed, into everlasting fire, prepared for the devil and his angels:

42 For I was an hungred, and ye gave me no meat: I was thirsty, and ye gave me no drink:

43 I was a stranger, and ye took me not in: naked, and ye clothed me not: sick, and in prison, and ye visited me not.

44 Then shall they also answer him, saying, Lord, when saw we thee an hungred, or athirst, or a stranger, or naked, or sick, or in prison, and did not minister unto thee?

45 Then shall he answer them, saying, Verily I say unto you, Inasmuch as ye did *it* not to one of the least of these, ye did *it* not to me.

.

46 And these shall go away into everlasting punishment: but the righteous into life eternal.

(Footnote 10) On climbing the wrong tree in the forest? Thoreau

"I went into the woods
because I wished to live deliberately,
to front only the essential facts of life,
and see if I could not learn what it had to teach,
and not, when I came to die,
discover that I had not lived.
I did not wish to live what was not life,
living is so dear,
nor did I wish to practice resignation,
unless it was quite necessary.
I wanted to live deep and suck out all the marrow of life,
to live so sturdily and Spartan-like as to put to rout all that was not life,
to cut a broad swath and shave close,
to drive life into a corner,
and reduce it to its lowest terms,
and, if it proved to be mean,
why then to get the whole and genuine meanness of it,
and publish its meanness to the world:
or if it were sublime, to know it by experience,
and be able to give a true account of it in my next excursion.
For most men, it appears to me, are in a strange uncertainty about it
. . ."
- Henry David Thoreau

(Footnote 11) Milky Way and hundreds of billions of galaxies?

(http://imagine.gsfc.nasa.gov/docs/ask_astro/answers/021127a.html and; http://seds.lpl.arizona.edu/Messier/more/mw.html)

There are hundreds of billions of galaxies. A recent German super computer simulation suggests as many as 500 billion. Our Milky Way galaxy which is the home of our Solar System together contains at least 200 billion other stars (more recent estimates have given numbers around 400 billion stars) together with their planets.

(Footnote 12) Fiddler on the Roof and Love of Wife and Husband?

(http://www.jpost.com/servlet/Satellite?c=JPArticle&cid=112774624155 9&pagename=JPost%2FJPArticle%2FShowFull)

"In the scene from Fiddler on the Roof, before the marriage of their daughter Huddle,Tevye asks his wife Golda and if she loves him. Golda, somewhat taken aback by the question, doesn't immediately give her husband the answer he seeks, but instead reminds Tevye of all the labors of love she has provided to him during their 25 year marriage such as cooking, cleaning, bearing and raising children, and even milking the cow. Nevertheless, Tevye, still not satisfied by Golda's responses, persists in asking his wife for verbal affirmation that in fact she does love him. Golda replies:

"For 25 years I lived with him, fought with him, starved with him, 25 years my bed is his, if that's not love what is?" Tevye responds: "Then you love me..." and Golda answers, "I suppose I do." Tevye responds, "I suppose I love you too!" Finally they sing together: "It doesn't change a thing but even so, after 25 years it's nice to know."

"It's nice to know is exactly the point. Couples get sidetracked and distracted by life's pressures and stresses such as job demands and making a living, raising and worrying about their children, taking care of aging parents, and for a new immigrant, adjusting to life in Israel.

"These pressures, instead of bringing couples together, often make spouses turn away from each other. They tune out and forget important dates, pick on their spouses over small and objectively insignificant things and show insensitivity to each other at the very times when a hug is called for.

"In time, they stop playing, laughing and communicating with or even touching each other. They tell themselves "this is the way most married couples live," which is, unfortunately, accurate. So they put aside romance and passion, settle for a functional relationship, and live semi-miserably ever after. They may stay together, but they don't stay intimate.

Dr. Mike Gropper is an American psychotherapist and marital therapist.

[Christmas Angel Picture taken from free Internet. No copyright or indication as to source is apparent.]

About The Author

Richard works at being a good husband, dad, grandpa, and neighbor. He is a Christian. He is a member of The Church of Jesus Christ of Latter-day Saints. He served as a Mormon missionary to the Netherlands, in the leadership of the Salt Lake Inner City mission, as a lay bishop, as counselor in two LDS stake presidencies and as Region Welfare Specialist. Besides writing, oil painting, gardening and golf, he is a businessman and attorney at law with a practice of business transactions, venture and debt capital. He was a vice president of Bonneville International Corporation and co-founder of the LDS Radio Network. He has met payroll. He owns his own company. He served as multi-county chairman of the Red Cross and as state chairman of The National Conference of Christians and Jews (and Muslims) and for thirteen years as a NCCJ national board member.

Some of Richard's other writings are: "Would Jesus Christ Do That?" is the first question!; 20 Ways To Make A Good Marriage Great; Essentials of Home Production & Storage; I Hope They Call Me On A Mission; and an LDS Welfare Services Handbook. Richard was co-producer and editor of The World's 100 Greatest Books 50 CD Audio Collection, The World's 100 Greatest People 50 CD Audio Collection, The World's 50 Greatest Composers Their Lives and Their Music 50 CD Audio Collection.

Author's Comment

"Be of good cheer" and "be not afraid" are comforting words of Our Savior. (Matthew 14:27)

We are children of God Our Eternal Father who hears and answers our prayers.

His Son Jesus Christ lives and will shortly come again.

A couple of websites you may find interesting include: www.lds.org and www.mormon.org. My Blog is http://jesus-isthechrist.blogspot.com/

To your great health, happiness, and prosperity!

Richard Linford.

A Sweetwater Book Company publication

www.ingramcontent.com/pod-product-compliance
Lightning Source LLC
La Vergne TN
LVHW081325060426
835511LV00011B/1869